For my heroes, who stood up to make the world a better place.
And for my husband, John, who makes *my* world a better place by standing beside me.
—E.E.

With gratitude to my fiancé and family for their love
—Z.C.

Visit us on the Web! rhcbooks.com

Educators and librarians, for a variety of teaching tools, visit us at RHTeachersLibrarians.com

Library of Congress Cataloging-in-Publication Data is available upon request.
ISBN 978-1-9848-3197-2 (trade) — ISBN 978-1-9848-3199-6 (lib. bdg.) — ISBN 978-1-9848-3198-9 (ebook)

Book design by Nicole de las Heras

Printed in the United States of America
10 9 8 7 6 5 4 3 2 1
First Edition

ENOUGH!

20 Protesters Who Changed America

Written by **Emily Easton** · Illustrated by **Ziyue Chen**

Foreword by **Ryan Deitsch,**
Parkland Survivor and Activist

Crown Books for Young Readers ♛ New York

Author's Note

A few weeks before the Parkland shooting, I was in Florida with my cousins for a family wedding. On Valentine's Day, a shooter went on a rampage at their school.

Thankfully, Samantha and her brother Ryan were both physically fine, though some of their friends, sadly, weren't. But everything changed from that moment on. Samantha was too young, but Ryan was part of the group that organized the March For Our Lives, and their older brother Matthew took a leave of absence from college to help the movement, too.

I felt inspired by these teens, like so many people did—and also felt a sense of wonder that my cousins were joining the public canon of activists who made important changes in our country.

I was moved to make a list of other protesters who stood up and said "Enough!" and was reminded that America itself was formed as a protest against England. Protest is part of America's DNA, and I wanted to share this realization in a book for young people. I especially wanted to show the many ways protesters have stood, marched, sat, or knelt for change in simple enough language for young readers to understand and feel inspired. Founding Fathers like Samuel Adams and new activists like my cousin Ryan have kept our country moving ever closer to its ideals. My hope is that their actions will inspire young people to find their own way to fight to make America better. Our country needs them.

—Emily Easton

Foreword

Whether I was doing a tight set at a comedy club, bussing tables at the local restaurant, or writing late into the night for the school paper, life was simple and senior year was almost over. Then a hurricane came through our town in the form of a lone gunman. People found solace from the pain in groups that aimed to make a difference. Some friends of mine came together hailing "Never again," and I was happy to add my voice. We demanded action and justice from a system that allowed children to be harmed in a classroom. We assembled our troops: students, teachers, parents, children, and even some politicians joined the fold—all to inspire hope and love to overpower our pain.

The key is inspiration; tragedy does not hold the only source. You can look to history for guidance and people like Dr. Martin Luther King Jr., Ruby Bridges, and the Freedom Riders of the civil rights movement, who all showed that peace and compassion go a long way toward creating balance in our society.

There's no telling how our actions will impact this world, but we are determined to continue our efforts to protect other communities from the horrors we faced. Anyone is able to join this fight; all you need is passion in your heart and a way to share it: online, in a crowd with a memorable sign, with something as small as a crayon or a pen. Anyone can help bring change. You can, too.

—Ryan Deitsch

Samuel threw a tea party.

Harriet led the way.

Susan cast her vote.

Woody sang for you and me.

Rosa kept her seat.

Ruby went to school.

Rachel wrote a book.

Martin had a dream.

Cesar and Dolores said, "No grapes!"

Muhammad refused to fight.

I AIN'T GOT NO QUARREL WITH THEM VIETCONG.

Tommie and John raised their fists.

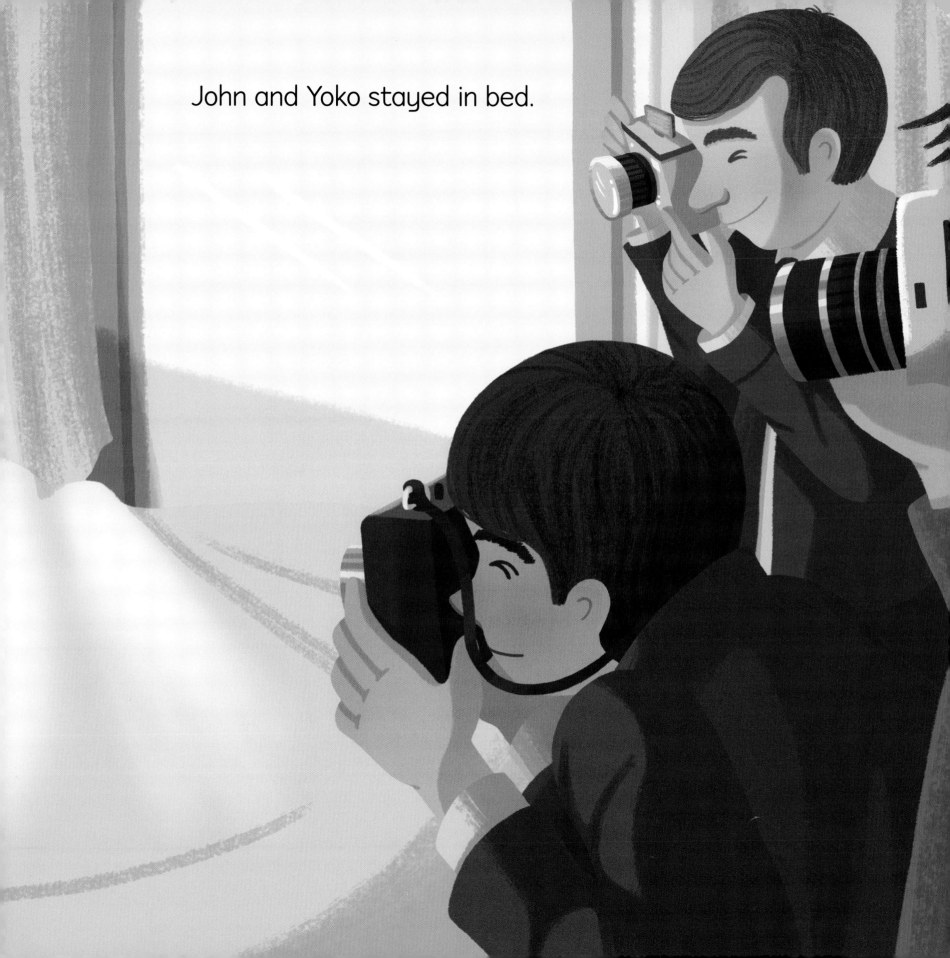

John and Yoko stayed in bed.

Gilbert sewed
a rainbow.

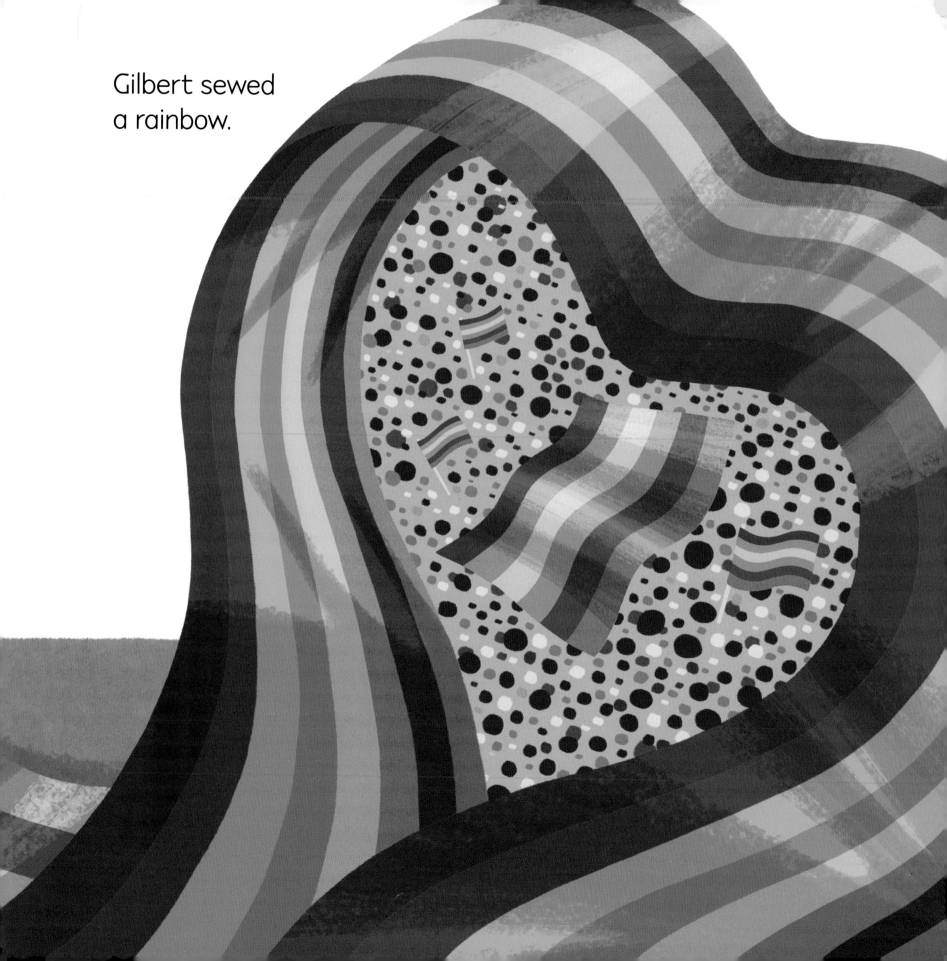

Jazz wore a dress.

Colin took a knee.

America said, "Time's up."

Parkland demanded, "Never again!"

Why These Protesters Said "Enough!"

SAMUEL ADAMS was a Founding Father and a mastermind of the Boston Tea Party, which took place on **December 16, 1773.** In the years leading up to the tea party, Adams helped establish the Sons of Liberty in protest of taxes imposed on the colonies by England, and coined the slogan "No Taxation Without Representation." These protests went from talk to action when Adams signaled to a group of patriots at a town meeting. They left, disguised themselves as Mohawk Indians, and boarded three ships to dump 342 chests of tea (worth almost one million dollars today) into Boston Harbor. The patriots' act of resistance was one spark of the American Revolution.

"This meeting can do nothing more to save the country!"

(The part of Adams's speech that is believed to have been his signal to the patriots.)

HARRIET TUBMAN escaped from slavery in 1849 and continued the fight against it by becoming the most famous "conductor" on the Underground Railroad. Though it is impossible to know the exact numbers, it is believed that **between 1850 and 1860** she returned to slave territory thirteen times, leading about seventy slaves to freedom—and gave information to many others so they could escape on their own. When the Civil War began, she used her skills to help the Union Army as a nurse, scout, and spy. Her activism never ended. In her last years, she added her voice to the women's suffrage movement.

"I was the conductor of the Underground Railroad for eight years, and I can say what most conductors can't say—I never ran my train off the track and I never lost a passenger."

SUSAN B. ANTHONY voted illegally in the presidential election on **November 5, 1872,** to draw attention to her fight for women's right to vote. She was arrested two weeks later, becoming the first person in the United States to be arrested and put on trial for voting. A judge found her guilty and ordered her to pay a $100 fine. She refused, expecting to be jailed, but the court let her go without paying the fine so there would be no more attention given to the issue. Susan devoted her entire life to the cause of women's rights, but she died fourteen years before the Nineteenth Amendment was ratified in 1920, which finally gave women the right to vote.

"How can 'the consent of the governed' be given, if the right to vote be denied?"

WOODY GUTHRIE wrote the song "This Land Is Your Land" on **February 23, 1940,** both to celebrate the wonders of America and to show that many Americans were blocked from experiencing them. He traveled around the country on foot and by rail, playing his songs to protest against corrupt leaders, fight for the underdog, and bring people together. These simple but powerful songs brought light to the darkness of the hard times caused by the Dust Bowl and the Great Depression and helped fuel the fight for labor unions against powerful bosses.

"It is a folk singer's job to comfort disturbed people and to disturb comfortable people."

ROSA PARKS was riding the bus on her way home from work on **December 1, 1955,** when she was arrested because she refused to give up her seat to a white person. She had been a civil rights activist for many years but hadn't planned her protest in advance. Her simple "no" to the bus driver that night sparked the Montgomery Bus Boycott. For 381 days, African Americans stayed off the buses, sharing rides or walking to work until the courts finally ordered the end of "Whites Only" seating on all city buses. This important victory for civil rights was won at great personal cost—both Rosa and her husband lost their jobs and had to move north to Detroit. But Rosa's sacrifice brought lasting change to our country, for which she received the Presidential Medal of Freedom and the Congressional Gold Medal.

> "People always say that I didn't give up my seat because I was tired, but that isn't true. . . . No, the only tired I was, was tired of giving in."

 RUBY BRIDGES faced daily threats and angry mobs when she became the first African American student to go to an all-white elementary school in the South on **November 14, 1960.** Every day, armed guards took Ruby to school to keep her safe. Many white parents pulled their children out of the school, and none of them allowed their children to be in Ruby's class. She spent all of first grade alone in a classroom with her teacher, Barbara Henry. Ruby's father lost his job and stores refused to serve her mother because they had sent their daughter to a white school. Even her teacher suffered: for the bold act of teaching Ruby, she was fired at the end of the year. But Ruby took that first hard step toward equality, and other brave students followed in her footsteps. Their actions, together with judges' rulings, brought an end to schools that separated people by the color of their skin.

> "Forgive them, because they don't know what they're doing."

 RACHEL CARSON wrote the book *Silent Spring,* which was published on **September 27, 1962,** and went on to inspire the environmental movement. The book revealed how chemicals called pesticides damaged the food chain, from the smallest insects to human beings. Rachel's ocean books had already brought her fame, and her fans quickly made *Silent Spring* a bestseller. Millions more watched Rachel share her scientific discoveries in a television interview, including President Kennedy. He created a Science Advisory Committee after reading her book, and those scientists agreed with Rachel's findings. Eventually, Congress passed laws limiting the use of pesticides. *Silent Spring* also led to the Clean Air Act in 1963, the Wilderness Act in 1964, the creation of the Environmental Protection Agency in 1970, the Clean Water Act in 1972, and the Endangered Species Act in 1973.

> "In nature, nothing exists alone."

 MARTIN LUTHER KING JR. shared his dream of equality and brotherhood for all on **August 28, 1963,** at the March on Washington for Jobs and Freedom, as part of his fight against racism in our country. He dreamed of a world where his children would "not be judged by the color of their skin, but by the content of their character." He dreamed of a world where different kinds of people could see themselves as brothers and sisters, instead of hating those who were not like themselves. About 250,000 people heard his speech live at what was then the largest demonstration in American history, and his message quickly spread around the world. Dr. King was an important civil rights leader who found peaceful ways to fight for change. The year after his famous speech, Dr. King was awarded the Nobel Peace Prize, the youngest person to receive the award at that time.

> "I have a dream that one day on the red hills of Georgia, the sons of former slaves and the sons of former slaveowners will be able to sit down together at the table of brotherhood."

 CESAR CHAVEZ and DOLORES HUERTA, cofounders of the National Farm Workers Association (NFWA), called for their union to strike against the Delano, California, grape growers, along with another union (AWOC), beginning on September 20, 1965. The strike was a way for powerless farmworkers to fight for better working conditions. These workers made very little money and had no toilets, no water, no medical care, no protection from pesticides—and no power. Even after six months of striking, the growers wouldn't agree to bargain with the workers. So Cesar and Dolores led strikers on a 300-mile march to the state capital in Sacramento. Then they asked Americans to boycott grapes. By giving up just one thing they enjoyed eating, they could help the poorest farmworkers in their fight. Millions of people stopped buying grapes, until the union signed an agreement on July 29, 1970, with twenty-nine growers, ending the strike and boycott.

> "*Sí se puede.* Yes we can." —Dolores Huerta

> "The whole essence of nonviolent action is getting a lot of people involved, vast numbers doing little things." —Cesar Chavez

MUHAMMAD ALI had been the heavyweight boxing champion for two years when he refused to be drafted to fight in the Vietnam War on **April 28, 1967,** because it was against his religious beliefs—and it cost him everything. He lost his championship, his right to continue to box, and possibly his freedom—if he lost his legal case. For years, Ali's lawyers fought in court to clear his name. On September 14, 1970, he won the right to return to boxing. Even though it was hard to get to the top again as an older, out-of-shape fighter, he won back the championship. At the same time, he had to continue his battle to stay out of prison for refusing to be drafted. Ali took his case all the way to the U.S. Supreme Court, where on June 28, 1971, he won in a unanimous decision. It was the biggest victory of his life. Ali left the sport in December 1981, the only boxer to win the championship three times. Though he had Parkinson's disease later in life and eventually lost the ability to speak, he became a UN Goodwill Ambassador and was chosen to light the Olympic torch in Atlanta in 1996.

"To those of you who think I have lost too much:
I have gained everything. I have peace of heart;
I have a clear, free conscience. And I am proud."

TOMMIE SMITH and JOHN CARLOS raised their fists in support of human rights on **October 16, 1968,** at the Summer Olympics in Mexico City. As they walked to the winners' podium to accept their gold and bronze medals, respectively, they took off their shoes to protest poverty in America. They each wore something around their neck to draw attention to lynchings of black people—Tommie wore a scarf, and John wore beads. John also unzipped his tracksuit in support of working people. They each borrowed a black glove from Australian silver medalist Peter Norman, who stood in solidarity with them, and raised a gloved fist. The crowd began to boo immediately, and both athletes were ordered to leave the stadium. The next day, Tommie and John had to return their medals, and both were suspended from the Olympic team. They later were banned from the Olympics for life. As time passed, people's view of this event changed. Their protest has become an iconic and respected moment in the fight for civil rights.

"We are black, and we are proud of being black."
—Tommie Smith

"If something is broke, I think every man, woman, and child should step up to the plate and try to have this thing fixed."
—John Carlos

JOHN LENNON and YOKO ONO turned their honeymoon into a Bed-In for Peace as a plea to end the Vietnam War. For seven days, beginning on **March 25, 1969,** a pajama-clad John and Yoko invited reporters and photographers to their bedside in an Amsterdam hotel room and talked about peace for twelve hours each day. The Beatles star and his new wife staged a second Bed-In on May 24 in Montreal, where they wrote and recorded the song "Give Peace a Chance," along with visiting celebrities. The song became an anthem for the anti-war movement and was sung by half a million people at the Moratorium March on Washington, D.C. John became such an effective voice for peace that the U.S. government unsuccessfully tried to have him kicked out of the country.

"We said, 'Let's get some peace, peace,
peace, peace on the headlines, just for a change!'"
—John Lennon

"Instead of making war, let's stay in bed."
—Yoko Ono

GILBERT BAKER called himself the gay Betsy Ross because he created the rainbow flag for San Francisco's Gay Freedom Day Parade on **June 25, 1978.** Harvey Milk, one of the first openly gay people to hold elected office in the United States, asked his friend Gilbert to create a flag for the parade because he knew Gilbert liked to sew. The first flags had eight hand-dyed colors: pink, red, orange, yellow, green, turquoise, indigo, and purple. Later flags dropped the pink stripe and combined the turquoise and indigo stripes into royal blue because those colors were too expensive to mass-produce. After Harvey Milk was assassinated, the flags were carried at the protests in his honor. LGBTQ communities embraced the brightly colored flag to show their pride in who they were and to declare to the world that they would no longer hide their true identity. The flag has become a symbol of LGBTQ rights everywhere.

"We needed something beautiful, something from us. The rainbow is so perfect because it really fits our diversity in terms of race, gender, ages, all of those things."

JAZZ JENNINGS wore a dress to her preschool's Dads' Night costume party on **April 20, 2006**—her first time dressing as a girl at school. Jazz had been wearing dresses at home from the time she was old enough to tell her parents that she was a girl, even though she was born with a boy body. But by the time Jazz turned five, her parents realized she couldn't be really happy unless she could be herself *everywhere.* Jazz was one of the youngest people to publicly identify as transgender, and she and her family have had to fight for her rights her whole life—including her right to wear a dress to school, to use the girls' bathroom, and to play on a girls' soccer team. As a teen, Jazz continues to be a trailblazer in the LGBTQ community.

"I've got a girl brain in a boy body. And I think like a girl, but I just have a boy body."

COLIN KAEPERNICK, quarterback for the San Francisco 49ers, knelt during the national anthem for the first time on **September 1, 2016,** to raise awareness about police brutality against African Americans. Other players began to kneel, too, and the protest started getting media attention. But at the end of the season, Kaepernick lost his job with the 49ers and has not been hired by any other team, despite his athletic ability. Players continued to kneel without him, and many players continue to support him and question why no owner will sign him for their team. He was given the *Sports Illustrated* Muhammad Ali Legacy Award for his courage and sacrifice.

"I am not looking for approval. I have to stand up for people that are oppressed."

AMERICA FERRERA joined Eva Longoria, Penélope Cruz, Zoe Saldana, and other Latinas along with more than 300 other women in Hollywood to found Time's Up on **January 1, 2018,** to support women who are hurt or held back by men in their workplaces. America and her group were inspired by a letter from 700,000 female farmworkers who wrote about being forced to do whatever they were told or risk losing the jobs they need to pay for food and housing. Time's Up has raised money for women to hire lawyers to fight back against men who use power or physical threats against them. In just the first sixty days, the Time's Up Legal Defense Fund had heard from 1,700 women working in over sixty different industries looking for help. America and the women of Time's Up are using their celebrity to bring attention to this problem so all working women can feel safe.

"We've got work to do for the next generation. Let's get to it."

PARKLAND STUDENTS survived a violent school attack, and just two days later, on **February 16, 2018,** they turned that tragedy into a movement that is fighting to make our country safer for schoolchildren—and everyone. Their outspoken demand that lawmakers find a way to protect people from gun violence has inspired the world. They organized the March For Our Lives, which drew 800,000 protesters to Washington, D.C., for one of the largest public demonstrations in American history. They also focused on registering new voters to try to elect leaders who support common-sense gun laws.

"Everyone's voices matter, and we want to help educate people and inspire them to speak up for what matters." —Ryan Deitsch

"Fight for your lives before it's someone else's job." —Emma González

"We have been silent for too long as a nation." —David Hogg